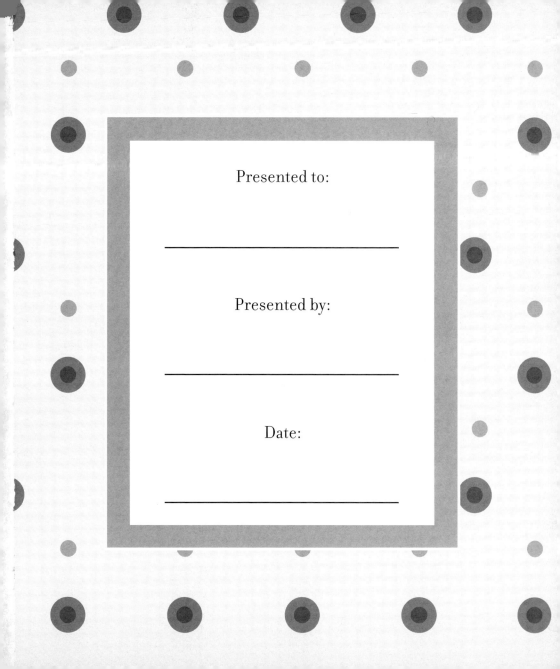

Presented to:

_____

Presented by:

_____

Date:

_____

For the
Love
of
Cats

A Delightful Photo Celebration
of Life with the Feline Kind

Cats are angels with fur.

- SARK -

Introduction

Independence, grace, and majesty all rolled into one ball of fluff. That is the Cat!

We love them for their independent nature—they do exactly what they want, when they want. Secretly, in our innermost thoughts, we would like to do the same.

And when they do decide to nestle up close to us, our hearts melt because we have been selected as their chosen person.

They're fun, playful, and have bounds of energy when they're awake! Cats are just too cool!

For the Love of Cats was created to celebrate the dignity and mystery of the regal feline, appreciated by emperors and royalty all over the world. We love them for their beauty, curiosity, confidence, and perkiness.

If you are blessed enough to have a cat to call your own, we know you will enjoy this sweet tribute to the magnificent, endearing, always adorable C-A-T!

All God's creatures carry
the footprint of His love…

But when God mixed fur with a purr,
He created a cuddly,
irresistible masterpiece.

A cat is heaven's way
of adding more love to your life.

When you give
your heart away to a kitty,
it's never lost.

Some of the best friends in life
are of the furry type…

And you can never have too many
feline friends.

The time spent loving your cat
is never wasted…

Even nine lives aren't enough.

There's just nothing quite like
a basketful of love.

Sometimes we all
need someone to lean on…

26

And who knows, love may be
as close as your front door.

So, when you find love is waiting,
don't hesitate to invite it in.

What are cats? They are hugs with tails.

To her, snuggling is not an option
—it's a necessity.

Inside him beats the heart of a lion—

yet on the outside
he can be sweet and soft.

Curiosity and playfulness met
when God created her...

But at times curiosity
has its down side.

Although he realizes practicing
generosity is sometimes difficult...

He knows the greatest gift
you can give is "yourself."

She will teach you that where there's a will,
there's always a way…

And remind you that the world
is filled with beauty and possibilities.

He always takes time
to smell the roses…

And he's never too busy
to take a vacation.

She faces each day with anticipation…

And is a reminder
that there's always adventure
to be found…

Even in the most unexpected places.

He understands what it's like
to have a day that ruffles your fur...

And he expects to get into a
tight spot every now and then.

But he knows God will always
help you land on your feet.

Her patience is a virtue...

And she has learned that
even enemies can become friends
over time.

She doesn't have any problem
getting in touch with her emotions…

And lets you know
that it's ok to be sad.

On those days when you need
a little comfort
and reassurance…

He'll encourage you to look up...

And get a whole new perspective.

She knows that sometimes life
is a real balancing act…

And you will feel stretched…

Squeezed…

And you may want to curl up
and hide.

Instead, take a little "alone" time…

Consider all your options...

Have the courage to take the first step…

Be a risk taker…

Then take advantage
of every opportunity.

When you're done, he'll be waiting…

Because when you have a cat,
there's just no place like home!

In Their Own Words

What cats would say
if they could talk

My Best Friend

Place your
cat's photo
here.

I love my cat because ...

_____

_____

_____

_____

_____

_____

_____

_____

_____

_____

_____

_____

Dogs come when they're called;
cats take a message and get back to you later.

~ MARY BLY ~

Do you have funny or heart-tugging pictures of your treasured pet? We would love to consider your photos for future inspirational pet books.

We need photos that are:
· In digital format
· At least 4 X 5 and 300 dpi

Submitting photos:
· Please email your photos to: petphotos@bordonbooks.com
· In subject line, put your last name and species of pet.
· It is helpful if you send one photo at a time.
· Include your full name, address, and phone numbers with area code.
· If you would like, include a one-line caption for the photo.

When your photo is accepted:
· We will ask you to sign a release for non-exclusive rights to publish your photo.
· We will send you a complimentary copy of the book in which your photo appears.
· We will credit you by name for the photo.

Thanks for your interest; we look forward to receiving your delightful photos.

Please email your photo to petphotos@bordonbooks.com

If this book has touched your life, we would love to hear from you.
Please send your correspondence (no photos please) to:
Editorialdept@whitestonebooks.com
Visit our Web site at: www.whitestonebooks.com

WHITE STONE BOOKS
LAKELAND, FLORIDA